WRIT

7 MANTRAS OF ORGANIC SUCCESS

---

*Living, working and changing radically
in the digital age*

All revenues donated to
Shree Rajendra Honeycomb Charitable Trust

Foreword by Brigadier Sushil Bhasin
Afterword by Jogesh Jain

Satish Purohit
Deepak Kotak
Deepak Kumar Singh
Sumit Sharma
Nara Subramaniam
Vijayalakshmi Raman
Jitendra Nath Mahato
J Lakshminarayanan

First Published in July 2020

Published By:
Kalon Maple Publishing
+91 9665 609 444

ISBN: 978-81-946591-4-3
Price: 299₹

Layout Design, Cover Design:
Mrunaal Gawhande

Distributed by:

Paperback: amazon.com, amazon.in, flipkart, pothi.com
E-Book: amazon.in/com, apple (ibooks stores in 51 countries), barnes &
noble (us and uk), scribd, kobo, and blio, overdrive (world's largest
library ebook platform serving 20,000 + libraries), baker & taylor axis
360, tolino, gardners (askews & holts and browns books for students),
bibliotheca cloud library (3,000 public libraries) and odilo (2,100
public libraries in north america, south america and europe) +
paperback

TABLE OF CONTENTS

7 MANTRAS OF ORGANIC SUCCESS

*Living, working and changing radically
in the digital age*

BY BRIGADIER SUSHIL BHASIN

Brigadier Sushil Bhasin is a time investment strategist, global speaker, and author of five books including 'Million Dollar Second' published by CNBC. He is a proud protégé of Speakers Institute. A TEDx speaker, and corporate trainer, he has a mission to create a world conscious of time as a vital resource. He delivers 'High Impact Virtual Engagement' webinars.
www.BrigSushilBhasin.com
sushil@BrigSushilBhasin.com

Foreword: Digital public speaking is the key

An outline of what it takes to profit from live global audiences online

By Brigadier Sushil Bhasin

I am delighted to write this piece, which precedes the literary efforts of nine stellar professionals who also happen to be my mentees. Let me admit here that I am happy for a rather selfish reason too. It is a known principle of communication that whatever is spoken first is easily recalled by the audience. I hope that is what happens with the words you are reading right now. I think it is appropriate that, I write on the confluence of my area of expertise as a time investment strategist, my focus on transition leadership and the art public speaking for pleasure and profit. I have also kept in mind that writers who follow me are alumni of the first batch of the Train the Online Trainer (TTOT) program.

The amazing bit is that the TTOT program was conceived, structured and executed entirely during the series of COVID 19 lockdowns and the participants are from all corners of India and the world. That Satish Purohit, my writing coach, was also able to take these new authors from the book-in-mind-stage to book-in-market stage in 21 days is amazing but then that is Satish for you.

We will now work towards making the book a bestseller across the world in print as well as kindle formats. We do it not just to ensure that your budding authors get a wide readership but to help do our bit for the Rajendra Honeycomb Trust.

They run an orphanage and an old age home at Bhayander in the Mumbai Metropolitan Region, India. The book is being handed over to the trust, which will gain all the revenues accrued from the sale of this book.

Time investment is the study of investing time in a manner that yields maximum returns. This concept allows us to numerically measure what we gain by any investment of time. The numerical value is expressed through the acronym ROTI (Return on Time Invested). The discipline of time investment was born shortly after the death of 'time management'. Time management is for managers operating in a relative static world. Time investment is for entrepreneurs operating in a world marked by constant disruption in the form of innovations in the brick-and-mortar as well as digital world. Public speaking is not something that needs to be defined here but there is definitely something to be said about public speaking through digital platforms. We don't call it public speaking. It is called a webinar at the moment but it is public speaking on   a digital platform   or digital public speaking. Whatever is it that you do for a living, and whatever you expect to achieve   through   public speaking,   there   is   no   ignoring the digital world for the world's millions trapped in their homes by COVID 19. So, here is a short introduction to what I have learned about digital public speaking.

Imagine operating at 10 per cent of your effectiveness: Nothing can replace the magic of a live audience in a hall with a stage topped with a mike at one end and the cheering, laughter and thunderous applause.

However, technology is fast catching up to create a virtual experience of public speaking that   approximates   the magic of speaking with a live audience offline.

Play with technology: I find Zoom to be an excellent platform to reach out to hundreds of people simultaneously today. It is cost-effective, easy to operate and also easy to monetize. A US based company, its patrons are spread across the world, which is a boon for public speakers. I am mastering the technology by playing with it and you should too.

However, the point here is that today it is zoom, tomorrow there may be even better platforms with improved features. It is important to stay updated, and the way to do it is to become children and play around with technology.

Create a home studio: This has to do with orchestrating the background that your audience sees. It makes sense to invest on what is effectively your podium from which you will address audiences across the world. I use a mobile camera, ring light and a Samson Q2U mic as the optimum value for money for a beginner. You are also going to need a flexible mobile holder to use a second device, tripod, headphones, and a green screen.

Dress for the occasion: We tend to go easy on ourselves when we work from home or address from home, which is a big mistake. Look your best self and ensure that your audiences like what they see especially when the camera magnifies your face. Protruding nasal hair or black heads can make the experience more unpleasant than it would if you were addressing an audience offline.

Train your voice: This goes for offline public speaking as well but there you have the luxury of using your hands and arms and also looking particular members in the eye to create connect. Physical proximity can cover in part the lack of voice modulation, resonance and throw. You have to learn to use the microphone well in a manner that you neither appear to be shouting nor murmuring into the mike.

The best speakers have an ability to make what they are communicating in a manner that resembles a communication. To approach a mike without training your voice is borderline criminal.

Use an expert to help you build your audience: The beauty of speaking online is that you are no longer confined to a particular geography and can actually find the right audience from Bandra to Burundi and from Andheri to Alaska. Engage a digital marketing expert who will guide you on how it is done.

Learn from the best across the world: This is an important lesson. Whether you are into public speaking for profit or pleasure, pubic speakers like Zig Ziglar, Sam Cawthon, Brian Tracy, and Anthony Robbins are all online today and so should you. Watch them, pay heed to how they go about it and learn from them. They are in the leaders in the speaking business and they are operating in the world's biggest economy that is also the home of Google, YouTube, Facebook, Twitter and Instagram. These are also people who are leaders in the art of responding to disruptive change. It helps that they are in the world capital of disruptive innovation.

Master the business side: Are you aware that billions of dollars are changing hands online and digital public speaking is at the heart of these transactions? You may or may not enter the business of using your public speaking skills to make money online but it can certainly be something that can help you open a new source of revenue for your existing business especially if you are a part of the coaching/ training/ facilitating/ consulting ecosystem. I have used the insights I am sharing with you in the last three months and generated more than satisfactory revenue. The quarantine has been very rewarding financially for me and for others. The skills that I have polished at various speaking platforms online and offline have been a big help.

Final four words to my digital public speaker friends in partial or complete incarceration in Corona Jail: Don't wait. Go online.

"It is never too late
To start with your idea."

---

7 MANTRAS OF ORGANIC SUCCESS

Living, working and changing radically in the digital age

BY SATISH PUROHIT

Satish Purohit is an author coach, writer, editor, journalist, and lyricist from Mumbai, India. He has provided value to brands like the Times of India group's Mumbai Mirror, Indian Express, Bangalore Mirror, Free Press Journal, Mid-Day, Crossword Bookstores, Ahmedabad Mirror, Granth Bookstore, Penguin Publishing, Jaico, CNBC TV 18, and Life Positive magazine, where he was deputy editor. He has also worked as a waiter, a cake salesman and factory hand at different points in his career. He is the co-author of the Patanjali Yoga Sutra Adventures.

Satish is an Economics graduate from the University of Mumbai.

satish.purohit@gmail.com

Preface: The path of the three snakes

On writing as a spiritual journey

By Satish Purohit

So, I will just dwell here on the spiritual dimension of 'telling' of which writing is a subset. The heart stuff. To begin with, there is fire – the desire to express, share, tell your story, write. This fire is fuel for your personal journey towards truth, your personal truth. You are born with natural curiosity. From the womb of this combination of curiosity and imagination is born desire or the fire. This is the fire to express what you have understood and the desire to ask the really big questions like 'What is love?', 'What is life?', 'What is death?' and so on. The questions seek to understand your personal truth in the context of life as you experience it.

The desire is the fire.

The ever-unfolding answers to your curiosity are facets of your personal truth. For fire to burn confusion and mental fog and to uncover the truth you need form. Form is the prism that gathers the heat of the fire and focuses it at one point. This concentrated heat burns the curtains of fog and reveals the truth.

Imagine what it would be like if the person you love deeply loved you right back. The energy of this imagination is fire. You want to express this fire by either talking about it to yourself or to others. Your contemplation of this person, his/ her specialness/ how and why he/ she makes you feel the way he/ she does is an exploration of truth, your personal truth.

Now, when you sit down to write a love letter, a song, an essay, novel or a Facebook post, you will have to consider the structure of an effective love letter, meter and rhyme in poetry, the ordering of points that your essay will cover, the story arc of your novel or the SEO parameters that will make your Facebook post reach most people.

Sentiment is not enough.

Sentimental, mental same thing.

The question 'How do I say this?' has to do with form.

Mastering a form, say a ghazal or a sonnet, allows you to express your telling in the most efficient or impactful manner. Form is the prism that intensifies your fire as it comes out of you. It is the vessel in which fire can be used to set others aflame. You can start with fire and align it to truth later and start working on form after that.

There are no set rules on which of the three you start with.

You can start walking on any of the three roads.

If you write just with a mastery of form, it does not move people.

If it is just fire that does not seek personal truth, it dissipates on its own and turns ineffective.

If it is fire without knowledge of form, it can dazzle only occasionally.

Fire, form and truth are three roads intertwined with each other like snakes making love. Be guided by the light of your personal truth shining like light at the end of the tunnel.

Wherever these three roads meet, magic happens.

Okay?

Your money supports these kids

Thank you for buying this book.

The ownership of this book has been handed over to Shree Rajendra Honeycomb Charitable Trust to support their homes for children and senior citizens.

The contributing authors continue to be sole owners of pieces authored by them. The authors are free to exercise their intellectual property rights by republishing, repurposing, rewriting or changing the format of the particular pieces authored by them in any manner they please. The rights do not extend to pieces authored by other contributing authors unless they have clear permission from those who have written the particular pieces.

Shree Rajendra Honeycomb Charitable Trust is an NGO dedicated to helping needy and abandoned children with a particular focus on providing health support, education and shelter.

Run by Shri Devendra Pratap Singh, the trust also runs a home for the aged called Samarpan on the Uttan Road, Bhayander, Mumbai Metropolitan Region.

The office and home for children are situated at Kharigaon in Bhayander. With the number of children increasing every year, the trust is looking for support from donors to move the children from the present facility, which is a property that is owned by his own family in a residential building. Shri Devendra Pratap SIngh may be contacted on the following address:

Shri Devendra Pratap SIngh
D-111 to 114,
Ostwal Tower No.1,
Opp. Lata Apt., B.P.
Cross Road No.4,
Kharigaon,
Bhayandar (East) -401105
District Thane
Mumbai Metropolitan Region
devendra_singh26@yahoo.com
Landline: 02228182230
Phone No: +919324789408
Phone No: +917208253488
Website: rajendrahoneycomb.org

7 MANTRAS OF ORGANIC SUCCESS

*Living, working and changing radically
in the digital age*

BY DEEPAK KOTAK

Captain Deepak Kotak is an original thinker.

The habit of looking deep into things and making deeper sense of what we usually miss, makes Deepak a great professional as a coach. His experience when he shares has a purpose which he is able to share in a way that others can relate to, and learn and apply. That is what makes his writings so relatable. There is always something for everyone. I am looking forward to what Deepak puts down on this episode.

Kaushik Banerjee,
Area Director,
IWG PLC

Chapter 1. Sailing to selling

My change of profession from merchant navy captain to sales trainer and performance coach taught me some powerful lessons on personal, professional and spiritual change for those considering a new life and a new career

By Deepak Kotak

Why am I writing this?

To share my story and inspire others to be bold in making conscious changes in their own lives. What I have learned is that if you keep an open mind and show some commitment and support it with a little planning, making big changes becomes easier. Around 1987-88, if anyone had asked me what I wished to become, they would have always heard me say 'air force pilot'. However, in September 1988, I found myself on a ship, which marked the beginning of my career as a mercantile marine. The details of that particular adventure is another set of stories for another time. The important bit that I wish to share here in this particular piece is that in all the years that followed I never ever dreamt that I would have a career in sales, much less in training and coaching people to sell better. However, a few decades on, here I am, doing just that. This is not just a story of my transition from sailing to selling but a phase of great learnings that are certain to add value to those who aspire to change boats midstream like me.

It was somewhere in the middle of 2004. I was just back from the US having completed my Masters in International Transportation Management, which was followed by a short internship with DHL Global Forwarding or DGF (then DHL Danzas Air & Ocean) under the Regional Sales Manager of the company in (We continue to be touch) New Jersey.

I was exploring suitable roles where I could learn something new and contribute with my existing skill set. The idea of doing my masters' was essentially a part of my effort to move from port to port. The internship with DHL did push me in a certain direction and while I was exploring a wider industry, interviewing with DGF India seemed to be an obvious choice. At first, though they liked the profile there did not seem to be a suitable opening, till one day, when I got a call from the M&S Head. I was asked if I could come across for a meeting. They were interviewing for a position that they felt matched my skill set. It was a position in sales. I was tasked upon to play an individual contributor's role of developing trade between partner countries and helping sales team at both ends. While I was obviously responsible for the results, I had no direct team under me, no direct reports directed at me to help me make informed decisions and no authority over either of the sales teams. Do bear in mind that I had recently captained a ship, had a team, had received direct reports, and possessed authority. All of this helped me navigate the route. Anyway, as I considered the role, one thing was obvious. I would need all the persuasion skills at my command to be successful in such a role. A good way to start would be to persuade the four people across the table that I fit the bill.

Given my background, they were not concerned about me handling an international environment. The good review from the RSM in US helped confirm this. They had but one key concern and a genuine one at that. "You have never done sales before this; how do you see yourself fitting into this role? How will you do this?" they asked.

It's been 16 years. I will do my best to recall my answer, which went something like this: "From what I know, sales is all about convincing someone to buy or use your product or service.

For the last 14 years that I have sailed, essentially on contract basis, I have had to convince companies that I'm the right choice and for the last two years that I have been teaching in the marine industry, I have developed a firm belief, that when I have understood something, I will find a way to make the person on the other side of the table understand it, whatever their level of comprehension might be (I was so confident about myself with respect to this one skill and I think this has helped me throughout my journey, both the skill, and my confidence in it). Your products and services cannot be rocket science. I am sure I can learn them, and when I do, I can convince anyone to buy them."

I feel the confidence with which I conveyed this message is what got them to give me a shot. Thus began my journey from a trade lane manager in 2004 to sales head in 2015, until when at the end of 2016, I ventured on another journey into potential exploration and development of people, through training and coaching through aUt sUr, (an acronym for – as you think so you are), which is what I call my training business company.

I think I did alright. I got a few promotions on the way and couple of awards too. There are clients from those days who are still in touch with me. Some still remember me for the work I did as a life science sector head for over five years after I had moved on.

Yes, I think I did alright.

Thank you for bearing with me this far. I thought a little background would help provide the context for our conversation on the subject of insights gained from my 'Sailing 2 Selling' journey. I call it conversation because I would love for you to reach out to me with your comments and questions, and with your own stories. Also, after reading this, when you wish to embark on similar journeys, you may have just found yourself a coach.

So, getting back to the story, it was only after I convinced my interviewers that I was the right guy did the reality set in.

That is when fear raised its head. I remember telling myself, "Bol to diya, karega kaise?".

"I have announced that I can do it but how will I?"

The habit of reading that I had picked up and cultivated while at sea helped. I read books on sales and selling (essentially Brian Tracy) to get a sense of the skill set and process. While each book had something valuable to offer - techniques, processes, tips, etc., essentially I found that they all built on a few key aspects like knowing your offering, understanding your client and their need, analysing and assessing the best fit, presenting your offering well and building a relationship with the client. I was also lucky that my company organised a sales training program a few months into my joining. I still remember the trainer with whom I remain connected enough for him to connect me with people I need to reach out to.

I have been a bull of sorts, a typical Taurean. Once I have decided on something, I will push my way through. So, now that I had made up my mind, bagged the role, in addition to reading up on sales, I did something that I strongly recommend to all my coaching clients today, a SWOT analysis. On hindsight, I know that it was not as good as what I am capable of doing today, but it was done reasonably well. I made an analysis of my strengths, skills, characteristics. I also looked at how I could superimpose them on the strengths and skills that I needed in sales.

Some of the skills, characteristics and learnings I had been fortunate to have in my journey thus far were – teamwork, persistence, building relations in a dynamic environment (Dynamic because members in my team were changing every month or so), interest and comfort with other cultures. I was not very observant though I thought I listened well. How wrong I was! Since, I have made a conscious effort to make this my best skill area. I also possessed a willingness to put in hard work.

I wasn't a fast learner. However, once I had understood something, I was able to find creative ways of explaining it to others who were struggling to make sense of the matter. I loved having many friends and still do. Being at sea allowed me to be comfortable with being alone. I had this strong belief that if I saw it, I could get others to see it. I was not very analytical and hated going through too much information (still do). I liked jumping into things and getting my hands dirty. I hated too much monitoring. I was open to instruction and comfortable taking orders from superiors up the line. I could also be a little defiant with them. I was empathetic with those down the line though. I could communicate well with people from different parts of the country and the world. I had noticed this about me; unless I needed sleep or had something important to work on, I would be itching to start a conversation with the person in the next seat on a flight or train.

I then reviewed the requirements of the role as I looked into the key aspects I uncovered from my reading and the sales training along with the basic sales process. To put it simply – Identify prospective clients, contact, understand need, analyze fit, present offering, follow up, negotiate closure, sustain relationship and business. My understanding of the entire sales engagement and process has developed a lot more since then and is much deeper today.

I was able to define the required skills, characteristics, and attitude as – extensive research and filtration (was terrible, hated it, hate it slightly lesser now). Reach out to unknown people and start a conversation or seek an engagement (cold calls). This called for boldness and the fortitude to stand being turned down. It helped that this was part of my role while I interned with DHL in the US. I would make cold calls and fix appointments for the sales team. The task involved empathizing, listening, and understanding the need of our customers. I had to understand my own offering more deeply. I had to comprehend the nature of the need of my customers and relate it to my own offering.

I needed to possess strong presentation skills to present my solution in the form of an attractive document followed by a focused explanation, which is still not a strength for me. I also needed persistence to keep following up. I also needed negotiation skills and to learn the art of closing the deal.

The was also the all-important task of building and sustaining relations, where there was business and where the business was yet to be secured or more or less lost. There were also other aspects like reporting activities, coordinating, and managing with stakeholders from various departments.

And of course, teamwork.

It is only when I sat peacefully and did my SWOT analysis that I realized that there were many areas where my existing skills and past experiences would support my new role. More importantly it allowed me to specify the areas of improvement and the need for new skill acquisition. This kind of sliced down the problem to manageable levels. It gave me much needed confidence, though there was still a lot to do. I do not believe I have all the requisite skills to reach peak levels yet. There are some aspects of the entire sales process and sales management with which I still struggle. However, I believe I raised myself to a reasonable level of expertise on most counts, which helped me eventually spend 12 years at various levels in sales in an organisation. Following that run, are my four years of selling my services as a trainer and coach under my brand aUt sUr.

One skill I unearthed in myself as I played along in my role was that of follow up. Honestly, I think this was biologically passed down to me by my mom. I have never met a more aggressive follow-upper than her in my life. People who make her a commitment have been known to shiver at her calls. This is an extremely useful skill and an important one to realise early in one's journey. The need is not for aggressive follow up but adequate, innovative, and well-timed follow up.

I am still learning, and taking mum's lessons forward. We are all slaves to our genes, right?

For a reasonable period, one of the things that troubled me was the lack of a team reporting to me. That I really did not have a team to call my own. Well I did, I just could not see it then. Until it dawned on me that a person is not on your team just because they report to you. They are on your team when they see that you have shared goals. Once I saw that, whilst still in my first sales role, which I held for about five years with the number or size of countries expanding (Eastern Europe, North America, South America...,), the effort I was putting in changed when I realized what a big team I had in reality. Now the entire sales team of India and the partner country were my team. It all depended on how many of them I could get to see the shared goal. How our success was mutually interconnected and how I engaged with them. I am still in touch with a lot of people from this phase of my life. My interpersonal skills that were honed at sea helped me considerably here. There was this one thing I used to do, and I highly recommend it to everyone. Every morning when I reached office, I would go around greeting as many people as I could, and I would stop over at a few desks (different) every day just to chat up for a few minutes. I do not have any proof of direct connection, but I do think this helped me get a lot of things moving when I needed to.

One thing that worked strongly in my favor was the fact that my company had an extraordinarily strong operations setup. We had some of the best product and operations teams in the industry. I had thought that because I had worked on a ship for many years, understanding freight forwarding would come to me naturally. Well, it did not. I had to work hard at understanding the product and the intricacies of logistics. Having a great product team and being open to learning from them helped tremendously. I was also fortunate to have started my career in sales with a boss who was so high on energy that you could feel him walk into the office.

If I did not hear the sound of his heel, I would say his energy and drive made him walk a few inches above ground. He pushed us and that was good. I also had a great set of peers across departments, and this was especially true of the sales team. Sometimes, I think our boss was a little scared that his team was so tightly knit, but secretly I know from the person he is, that he would have it no other way. I think this was another important lesson for me. Peers can be great friends in competition. Being open and receptive to experts only increases your own knowledge and also strengthens your skill set further.

Well, all was not and is not hunky dory. I did make many mistakes along the way. Some I am sure I have not realized till date. There were few that I believe had a significant impact on me. I am keen to share those with you. The learning might come handy, especially if you are looking to make a similar journey:

- The ability to understand the feedback you get is extremely important. To proactively ask questions on the feedback so you have clarity for action and knowing which feedback to work with and which to ignore. One feedback I received often, in fact, in every annual appraisal for the first few years was that I was not aggressive. Had I chosen to; I could have demonstrated aggression. However, I never really understood the feedback and I could not identify myself as an aggressive person. So, I did what I do well, I resisted (I am a bull, remember?). I strained my relationship upward for a while, till one day I had the good fortune in another training organised by my good company, where eventually I learnt the difference between 'aggressive behaviour' and 'assertive behaviour'. Game changer. A tipping point of sorts (Thanks, Suhail!). I understood what my boss really wanted was more assertive behaviour.

I realized how being more assertive would make me more effective, as a person, as a colleague, and as a salesperson. When I understood assertive behavior, I was able to see myself being assertive and so started the journey to being assertive. If only I had clarified and got more specifics on the feedback, I may have made better progress and not lost out on those few years.

- I had not prepared myself for the 'no's', I never even thought about it. I had heard no, many a times in life, but the number of no's you hear as a salesperson is something else. I believe this should be an imperative part of every basic sales training, whether you call it handling objections, rejections or just managing the No. One of the things that saps a salesperson's energy in their early years is dealing with rejections. Until they find their own way to get charged up every time, they can either treat a 'no' on face value and feel dejected or reframe the 'no' as a gift. I thought this took a lot. I think when a salesperson tips over this point that he/she genuinely comes of age. I have heard and read that a huge number of people give up sales in the first year for the single reason that they are unable to handle the quantity and frequency of the 'nos' that are thrown at their face. A 'no' does sap my energy even today, I will be honest. I have however found ways to manage them better by sometimes seeing them as a gift. Sometimes as opportunity and at other times by detaching myself from the no and realising that the rejection is for the offer and not for me. I tell myself that my map is not yet aligned to the needs of the clients.

- Managing people upwards is important. I'm not sure I'm the best person to give advice on this subject. I can tell you that managing your bosses (no one has one boss anymore) is a skill you must develop early into your career.

It may sound negative at first but when you are able to see that your boss has the potential to be the biggest hurdle and biggest opportunity for your growth, you start understanding the importance of managing them. When I say manage them, what do I mean? Essentially that you keep in mind that they are extremely important stakeholders in your work journey, and it would make a big difference to your life if you are able to empathize with them and create a situation where they can empathise with you. If you can manage this bit, the outcomes will be amazing. That your success is their success is not always obvious, and you must ensure there is absolute concurrence on that. You want to have your boss want your success as badly as you want it. While practicing emotional intelligence is a great skill to help you here, your first step must be to create the right mind-set or mind-frame around your bosses. For me this is still WIP. Fortunately, for the moment I am my own boss and, of course, so is every client of mine.

- You do not have to be and most likely will not become the best in every facet or stage of the sales process. Find out early which stage comes naturally to you. This can become the core around which you would enjoy developing yourself. Find ways to fence your weak areas or areas that you do not enjoy much. You can use will and motivation to become good enough there or find a partner where both complement each other. While I sincerely advice you not to ignore your weaknesses, please do not spend too much time on becoming excellent on your weak areas. Be innovative to find alternatives. Spend as much of your time becoming better in the areas of your strength. These are the ones that will make you win.

One of my biggest learnings on this journey have been the kind of relations you build as you go along with both, your internal and external clients.

It is important that your relations are such that when they think of you, they think of you fondly more often. When people like you they will also like doing business with you. One of the best ways I have found to get people to like me, is to find reasons to genuinely like them. While my journey is from sailing to selling, yours may be across different waypoints and inspired by different objectives and goals. Yet, there will be parts of our journeys that look alike. I hope some paths that I have charted, allow you to make a better passage. Imbibing learnings from some of my successes and mistakes might help you avoid certain obstacles and fast track your journey.

It was the Diwali of 2016, many years after I initiated the journey from 'Sailing 2 Selling', that I initiated another journey, from 'Selling 4 Others to Selling 4 Self'. This took birth in the form of aUt sUr Interventions and Transformations where in addition to coaching people for performance enhancement, and conducting leadership workshops, I also conduct customized sales workshops built around a structure I call 'Coach Kotak's 7P process'.

Having travelled a good part of my life to over 70 countries, I have had the good fortune to cross many paths. Maybe, one day ours cross too. Maybe, the crossing would just be by the way of this book. Maybe, after I have shared a bit of myself through these words, you will reach out a hand to shake mine, and we will be friends and learn from each other.

Summary of insights:
1. Take deliberate decisions: The right and wrong of decisions is always in hindsight and debatable. Know that eventually it is always your choice.
2. Respect the power of relations: When you find reasons to like people you will be connected longer. Seek mentors and coaches, they are all around. Identify key stake holders early with a 360 view.

3. Consistently raise self-belief: Raise awareness using a process that works for you. Connect to your resourcefulness. Create propelling beliefs. For me it was my belief that anything I had understood myself, I could convey to others by putting myself in their shoes.

4. Submit to learning: Consistently develop your knowledge and skill, with a will to excel. Feedback is a great way to learn. Develop this skill early. Sharpen your skills and fence your weaknesses.

5. Shared goals make teams: Nothing brings people together better than shared aspirations. Do not allow org charts and dotted lines to limit you. You will not be the best at everything, you will need a team. Collaborate.

6. Feeling rejected is a choice: Every idea has the potential for rejection, not just yours. The rejection for your effort is just feedback to review the effort or idea.

7. Even inspiration demands perspiration: A passionate hard worker just does not notice the perspiration. Once you are convinced of your direction, stay persistent.

Coach Kotak as he is now fondly known aspires to play catalyst in igniting journeys towards wholesome living, through wholesome performance. He endeavours to achieve this by helping clients explore their potential and aspirations and partners to co-create their road-maps towards success and happiness. He has played professional roles of ships' Captain, Tutor, Sales Specialist, and continues playing the roles of Trainer, Facilitator, Consultant and Coach. He is also an aspiring author taking his first baby step with this effort. Coach Kotak is a certified Trainer & NLP Master Practitioner, an ICF ACC credentialed coach and a certified Inner-MostShift coach. His underlying principle in exploring human potential is 'as you think, so you are' which is reflected in the name of his proprietary company 'aUt sUr'...

All rights of this chapter held by Deepak Kotak

7 MANTRAS OF ORGANIC SUCCESS

*Living, working and changing radically
in the digital age*

BY DEEPAK SINGH

Deepak Singh is an inspirational leader. He has shown great grit and determination in attaining his pursuit of life. I have known Deepak for 15 years now. He has been a friend, a colleague and a competitor of mine. I must admit, I have not known many others who have shown such perseverance towards moving ahead towards his goal in life. Deepak has always smiled away the hurdles in his life and has overcome them victorious. I appreciate him so much for his genuity, innovativeness and dexterity. He has emerged as a confident, spirited and compassionate entrepreneur. I am sure Thela MBA will give all a hands on perspective on entrepreneurship and innovation.

Gesu Shekhar,
Founder and Director, Eloquence!

Chapter 2. My MBA in thela entrepreneurship

Business insights gathered from running a rolls and wraps food cart in Patna after 09 years in the corporate world

By Deepak Kumar Singh

It was my very first day. I was about to throw my food cart open to business. I was excited and nervous. The year was 2016. All four of us – the chef, his helper, the thela or food cart, whom I count as a team member and I – were present at the site. My thela was an e-rickshaw, which I had converted into a food cart at a garage in Patna. It was very first e-rickshaw-turned-food cart of Patna. The remodeled e-rickshaw caught everyone's attention on the road. I was very proud of the thela only as a parent can be of a child.

So, coming back to that very first day, I reached 'my spot', which I had chosen after two months of a very tiring search. It was an area frequented by students with deep pockets and affluent residents. It was an upmarket area of Patna, and in my opinion the perfect location for selling fast food. I had managed to 'ease into' this place with the help of a friend's relative, who had a permanent shop in the neighborhood and was well respected in the market there.

Once all things were set, we parked our e-rickshaw on the other side of road as a few rickshaw pullers were relaxing on their rickshaw at the location, where my food cart was supposed to be parked. Hours passed but my thela remained parked on the opposite side. A day passed and we were unable to convince the rickshaw pullers to move despite calling my friend's relative to use his considerable influence.

The space was a *rain-basera* or night shelter of rickshaw pullers and they used to use that space to park their rickshaw after sunset. They were clear that they would not allow a food business to run at the location.

I was flabbergasted. My dreams were getting shattered before my eyes. It made me very nervous. I had no idea what I would do next. I wondered how I would get a new space to run my moving restaurant. I did not want to reveal my nervousness to my employees who had thrown their lot with me. I decided that it would be a good idea to lie to them so they did not abandon me.

"Don't worry, I have few more back up locations. We will start our business from there," I told them.

That night, I slept very badly and after a lot of tossing and turning. However, God was kind. A relative came to my rescue. It did take me 20 days but I finally found space in a very high foot-fall area of Patna, which was far better than the previous location. I want to tell anyone who plans to start a business to not stop believing in oneself or on God. The rest will surely follow. If anything is taking time, there is a bigger purpose behind it. It is for your betterment. Just keep trying, and do your best. Leave the outcome to the almighty. Rest assured that he will take care.

Corporate to street vending

It was 11.00 pm and we were about to retire for the day. Suddenly, my wife felt a pain in her stomach. Within half an hour, the pain grew uncontrollable. She came close to fainting. There was nobody else in the house. I was not in a position to leave my wife alone to go downstairs to hunt for a cab or an auto rickshaw. This was before Ola or Uber opened shop in India. I didn't have a car back then. She was not in a position to ride pillion on my two-wheeler to the doctor. We had shifted recently to the apartment. I did not know the neighbors. I called one of my senior office colleagues who lived nearby.

He was kind enough to drive his car to our house and ferried us to the hospital where my wife was admitted. The doctor informed me next morning that there was an infection in the stomach. He asked if she had eaten any street food that day.

The aaloo chaat and paani puri she had that evening was to blame.

I am also a foodie who enjoys street food. I have had my share of feelings of heaviness, acidity and burning sensations after eating out. However, nothing as severe as what my wife was experiencing had ever happened with me. The incident changed me.

That night as I waited in the hospital with my wife, I told her that, I would one day start my own street food joint. I would bridge this gap between taste and health. Food I served would have great taste and it would not make people sick but would contribute to their health. This seed of marrying taste to health took many years to take root but happen it did! I am happy that I am finally offering fresh, hygienic, tasty and healthy food to all my customers.

So, coming back to the story, here I was!

An MBA with nine years of experience in the corporate world, selling rolls with spicy fillings by the roadside. I left the comforts of an air-conditioned office that I had grown accustomed to and followed my passion. It wasn't easy for me. I had the distinction of being the very first person in our extended family to start a business. The fact that I was starting out from a thela was embarrassing to many of them. Selling food from a cart on the road after earning an MBA was not something children from respectable families did.

But then, I had made up my mind. My own family understood and supported me. I was careful to not get trapped in the 'Log kya kahenge' (LKK) or 'What will people say?' syndrome. I started my business with a small investment. After some effort, we celebrated our second 'first day' opening of our thela.

We decorated our shop with flowers and conducted a trial run with the staff before the launch.

After having worked on branding, logo, visibility, pricing, competition mapping, food quality, menu and taste. I was ready to conquer the market with my superlative wraps and rolls

My elation was however short lived.

To my surprise, nearly nobody was buying from us. People would look at the thela and go their way. Very few people actually bought my rolls on day one. I did a sale of Rs.460 only on day one, which was very discouraging. However, I didn't allow myself or my team to get disheartened. It was just the first day. The days that followed were not too encouraging either. I kept working on offering fresh, hygienic and tasty food to my customers. I made sure that I was engaging all my customers by talking to them. I made effort to know them. I also encouraged them to give their feedback to us. Despite all my efforts, my sale did not cross Rs.500 a day even after a week had passed since the opening.

On the 10th day, a customer suggested that I introduce a new item and create a combo offer. I liked the suggestion and implemented it on that very day. It began raining customers and within 3 days, I discovered that my sale had increased by 900 per cent compared to the 10th day. Since that day, the 13th, there was no looking back. My sale JUST kept on increasing day by day.

Please note that swimming can't be learnt by standing on the banks and looking at other swimmers. It is only after you jump into the water that you discover ways to swim through the swift river of challenges.

The lessons that I had gathered along the way were many. Here are some of the key learnings of my 'thela MBA' that could inspire you to take new risks and create your personal fortune:

1. **The desire to succeed is the key to success**: After two weeks of swatting flies at the thela, there came a point when there were more customers at my shop that I could

handle. I had a waiting time of 15 to 30 minutes at my outlet. Almost 15 to 20 customers were always waiting at the outlet to get their order. This is when I was paid a visit by the 'Halla Gaadi' or the Patna Municipal Corporation's hawker clearance squad paid me a visit. Having worked in corporate world, I had no idea of the government formalities and permissions required from the PMC in order to start street vending business. They were tasked with riding the city of unauthorized street vendors. They would come with their big trucks, seize the carts and other belongings and also impose hefty fines on the unauthorized street vendors. All the unauthorized thela shop owners were running here and there with their thelas.

It was a chaotic scene.

The authorities imposed a fine on my shop. They also made me shut my shop and warned me to keep it closed till I had completed all the formalities. Looking back, this incident made me think that, everyone was saying that getting government approvals is a very difficult task. It could take one year or more.

"How do I get the approvals?" I asked myself.

My mind was swimming with all kinds of questions. But then, this was a fight for my existence and my dreams. I was determined to get the required approvals come what may. I ran from pillar to post. Paid a visit to all the concerned authorities and told them about my dreams and passion of starting my food business. I had a trust in the process. I followed the guidelines diligently. Though it took me some time, I finally obtained all the required documents.

In this journey, I sought help from people who were complete strangers and to my surprise they helped me generously.

Ask for help and be prepared to take on challenges. A problem that appears much bigger in the beginning gets small, when you actually make up your mind to face it. Don't work from a fearful mindset. Believe that you can manage everything and anything in

life. This only comes from doing it repeatedly with the right mindset and a desire to succeed.

2. **Handling competition:** My shop was well-known in the neighborhood in the three months that followed. My success attracted the jealousy of fellow thela operators. They began to bad mouth my business.

"Don't you eat there! They don't serve fresh food," one of them said. They began to pick up fights with me on a daily basis on small issues and they chose peak business hours to do it. They even tried to poison the ears of my employees and failing at that started disturbing them in my absence. The plan was to harass them into quitting my employ so my business would collapse. Then a competitor decided to clone my shop. This disturbed me and I feared that I would lose my customers.

But then, there is a saying: "We don't grow when things are easy, we grow when we face challenges." I decided to rise up to the challenge by focusing on offering fresh, hygienic and tasty food to my customers. The clone closed in two months, and all my neighbors understood that I was here to stay. They would get kicked in the face if they disturbed my business. These incidents made me stronger, and more resilient.

The thela helped me come of age.

I learned more 'duniyadari' or street smarts from my thela than the two years invested in getting an MBA and my corporate exposure of 09 years. My MBA made me a manager but my experience at the thela made me an entrepreneur. Now, in the four years I have run the thela, I have expanded and ventured into other business as well. I find that I am capable of taking more risks. I can do whatever I feel like doing in my life. This is the result of my MBA earned in the last four years on the thela, which continues to teach me new lessons every day.

How many rolls should I wrap for you?

Key insights from my thela entrepreneurship journey

- ➢ Plans are neat, life is a way messier. Anticipate challenges along the way.
- ➢ You have to keep hustling, improvising and keep creating new offers before you strike gold.
- ➢ Be a market leader by making micro improvements every day so that your competitors are left breathless and your customers appreciate the extra.
- ➢ Remember there is toil between seeding and reaping a harvest. You have to wait for the season of success and till you have to keep hustling and try different things till something connects.
- ➢ Nothing will prepare you for it other than actually doing it. Every location is different. Every new thela is a new MBA.

Deepak Singh is an entrepreneur working on a mission to "Make India Healthier". He is an MBA from the Indian Institute of Technology (ISM), Dhanbad. His education was followed by nine years in leading multinational companies and four years in the restaurant business.

His life goal is to serve customers with healthy and tasty food. Starting from a small food cart, he has upgraded his business, which includes a takeaway restaurant today. This book talks about the entrepreneurial lessons learnt from four years in the food business. When not absorbed in his mission, Deepak pursues meditation and self-healing.

He lives in Patna, with his wife, parents and two children.

singhkdeepak@gmail.com

7 MANTRAS OF ORGANIC SUCCESS

Living, working and changing radically in the digital age

BY SUMIT KUMAR SHARMA

Sumit Kumar Sharma is an engineer in Electronics and Communication, MBA in HR, and an IT professional with 13 years of Industry exposure to the IT & Telecom sector. He has a declared vision of transforming rural India.

sumitksharma2020@gmail.com

Chapter 3. Dripping water, melting cheese

Lessons for change ninjas from Israel and Switzerland for creating village economies in India that are self-sufficient, self-sustainable, and abundant village economies in India that halt rural-to-urban migration and serve the interests of the rural worker who is mistakenly being called an unskilled labourer.

By Sumit Sharma

Becoming self-sufficient is of utmost importance, and if this self-sufficiency can be achieved in villages that are self-sustainable, it is like having a cake with a cherry on top. The term self-sufficiency is misleading because as social beings, we humans live interdependent lives. For an individual, a family or a tribe or clan to be self-sufficient, the village, town or city has to be self-sustainable. Joseph Stowell was probably thinking along these lines when he said, "Perhaps the greatest self-deceit is to tell our-selves that we can be self-sufficient." In the ultimate sense, we cannot be self-sufficient as individuals; but as a society, it is an achievable goal for a village, town or habitation.

Mahatma Gandhi recognized that India lives in its villages. This is largely true even today. Gandhi advocated development of self-sufficient villages. Had we listened to him; we could have stemmed the rural-to-urban migration a long time ago. Overnight skilled workers in the farms become unskilled laborers in the city; they have nothing to offer beyond basic labor. Today, a farmer's son may not want to be a farmer and a metal worker's son does not want to be a coppersmith. This is rightly perceived as freedom from the stranglehold of caste, but there is another perspective from which readiness to abandon traditional occupations may be viewed.

If these farmers, skilled workers and artisans could be supported by finance, technology, and an upgraded education that permit them to supplement their traditional knowledge, these farmers would be in a better position to compete in the nationwide market and even abroad. Had such efforts been made and our villages become self-sufficient to some degree, we would have been a more prosperous nation.

University of Delicious Cheese

Every region has its own unique characteristics and resources, which indicates the route we take to develop the ecovillages situated therein. Within the region, one ecovillage can depend on another based on its particular niche so that a self-sustaining mini-economy is created right there. With sufficient upgradation and infusion of finance, these villages can also supply their produce, goods and services to the entire state, nation and even internationally like the Swiss do with their cheeses. In creating such mini-economies, we should bear the African proverb that tells us how "the Sun does not forget a village just because it is small". We can identify niches within these regions through remote sensing techniques via satellite as well as through studies on the ground that take factors like geography, topography, climatic conditions, soil and water into account.

I mentioned the Swiss earlier. Switzerland is a classic example. They understood that they did not have many resources excepting dairy. That is what they focused on along with tourism. They also developed Switzerland as one of the most reputed financial destinations in the world. We need similar customized local solutions for our rural areas to build healthy communities that can create prosperous lives for themselves and for the nation at large.

Cambridge to Uttarakhand

Developing human resource through upskilling and supplementary learning is the key here. This is the next hurdle. We need to identify existing skills and resources to start with.

Recently, Prof Ronita Bardhan of the Indian Institute of Technology Bombay and Ramit Debnath from the University of Cambridge proposed a model for utilizing available resources in an Indian village to generate self-sustaining livelihoods and facilitate rural development. A framework was conceptualized in three phases resource mobilization by obtaining the necessary resources from the producer, bricolage (Construction or creation from a diverse range of available things) for village development and implementation of existing government schemes. Such activities need to be undertaken in all village clusters in the identified region as well so that low impact sustainable living can be created for all of them.

Following a study into what skills are required in the growing micro economy, it is a good idea to help workers upskill in the identified areas. Workers as well as micro entrepreneurs should be encouraged to acquire fresh skills that help them benefit from new opportunities being created as a result of government initiatives or local cooperative movements. The movement calls for a coherence between what is already there and what one needs to build. Gone are the days when imparting training was a costly affair due to the language barrier. Today, we have channels like YouTube that allow us to create educational audio-visual clips that may be utilized and broadcasted widely in the language spoken in a particular area to help villagers grasp new knowledge quickly and efficiently.

Lessons closer home

If people pool their resources and form cooperatives as has been done successfully in Maharashtra and Gujarat, study groups can be planned to foreign countries that have been successful in the identified areas of economic activity. Israel, I believe, is one such country to learn from in this respect. They are pioneers who gave the world 'drip irrigation' along with several eco-friendly greenhouse technologies that have created miracles in the Israeli desert. Closer home, we have Auroville in the Southern part of India, which was established in 1968 with the spiritual objective of embodying the ideal of human unity. The village has a philosophy of considering our biophysical reality as an evolutionary expression of the spirit. Auroville Eco Village has become world-class leader in its compressed-Earth building methods, harvesting of rainwater, plant-based sewage treatment plant technology in addition to harnessing solar and wind technology.

There is another eco-village named Kanda Jakh in Uttarakhand where a portion of the village land has been designated for agriculture. This land feeds all the people of the village with organic biodynamic produce. The landscape is designed based on the ease of access considering the availability of natural resources such as water spring flow. Homes are designed in such a manner that 30 percent of the energy requirements are fulfilled directly by solar power. The use of solar panels for electricity and solar heaters for hot water is widespread. This fulfils 60 percent of their energy requirements. The villagers also have special focus on water management. This eco-village will very soon be a model village where trainings will be provided to others helping them replicate this model of a self-sustaining village. One thing in terms of technology common to almost all eco villages across the world is the 'closed circular loop'. This loop is created by turning waste from one system into input for another system. Additionally, the Indian Government's Skill India Platform can be used to impart such training where such visits can be scheduled.

In order to create such ecosystems, easy access to rural loans for those who want to either start afresh or upscale their existing business is a must. Connectivity to the larger market is also an area that has to be looked into. It has been observed that after serving the community, these eco villages create surpluses that can be sold in the market to generate additional revenue. With the help of the government, new colonies can be setup with industries nearby to support such eco-villages and in collaboration they can fulfil each other's needs. With the support of NABARD and other agencies Co-operative societies may be set up. Experts like James Ehrlich who left his job to film organic producers and eventually went on to set up many eco villages across the globe. We would do well to learn from his concept of eco village, which incorporates concepts like 'healthy communities,' 'organic and biodynamic family farming,' 'food forest' 'farm to table,' and 'energy positive homes.'

Save Mother Earth

To conclude, self-sufficient and self-sustainable communities connected with each other in the form of a chain are the need of the hour. Each village will function as a link in the chain of this community of eco-villages that will be connected to similar other villages in the vicinity. Together, all villages comprising different communities will form a single umbrella super ecosystem that will strive to maintain progressively higher equilibrium levels without external help. Employment can be facilitated to the so-called 'un-skilled' and the 'skilled worker' alike. What is more, these workers can find gainful employment in their own niche once they are empowered with technology, training and modern techniques. This will help them in improving not only their socio-economic status but also with new tools and techniques to conserve nature as well. Maxime Lagace famously said, "by discovering nature, one discovers oneself." All progress, therefore, begins with a close look at what we already have in nature around us. Our organic reality should be the foundation on which we build a strong, happy and abundant India.

A connected chain of eco-villages is certain to provide a fertile ground for the birth of a new breed of social entrepreneurs that will create a lasting prosperity aligned with nature.

The Intergovernmental Panel on Climate Change has declared that 'Nobody on this planet will be untouched by the impacts of climate change.' A study released by Nasa had warned that Global Industrial civilization could collapse in the next 30 years due to resource exploitation if we continue living the way we have been for some years now.

Mother Nature is sending us repeated warnings. Let us wake up from our slumber and mend our ways. Let us do it before it is too late.

All rights of this chapter held by Sumit Kumar Sharma

7 MANTRAS OF ORGANIC SUCCESS

*Living, working and changing radically
in the digital age*

BY NARA SUBRAMANIAM

Fascinating first chapter. **Nara,** you have started most
appropriately with mother, father and teacher. Your
recollection of interacting with the seven sources of influence
in your life is remarkable. I now wait to read your other chapters.

Dato' V. L. Kandan,
Formerly of Shearn, Delamore & Co.
Malaysia

Chapter 4. Lighthouses for champions

*I owe my life, my knowledge, and my success
as a business coach to insights imbibed from my seven
Gurus whose teachings, integrity and personal examples
continue to guide my thoughts, emotions and professional
practice.*

By Nara Subramaniam

Like pots shaped on the wheel of time by many potters, we bear the imprints of all the hands that shape us. These are our enlighteners, our Gurus. I am no exception to this rule. I have been, and continue to be guided to higher levels of creativity, efficiency and abundance by my teachers. In this chapter, I offer my gratitude to some of them beginning with my parents, my very first and most influential teachers, the first and original two sources of all I know. Parents are our first university and we learn from them through an organic process of osmosis. It would take me a few volumes to fill you in on the multi-faceted personalities these Gurus possess and I fear that I might not be able to do justice to the immensity and depth of their wisdom.

Mother, my first guru

The common thread that contributed to the success of my career of almost five decades was what I learned from this one person. She certainly takes top honors as my primary guru. She was someone who touched the hearts of everyone she ever met. The depth and breadth of her love, care and giving knew no bounds. Someone with limitless energy and enthusiasm, her day always had more than 24 hours. Someone with a passion for living, she loved everything she did, be it cooking, singing, teaching music, gardening, entertaining or making friends.

She was someone who countered the negativities of life by doing something good for someone, somewhere, somehow. In hindsight I find that all through my life, since the age of my earliest awareness, all that my mother advocated has resonated deeply with my instincts, habits and decision making process.

Further reflection reveals that she helped me cultivate grounded attitudes and behaviors that made me an employee any employer would give an arm and a leg for. I have held dear to my heart the values she inculcated in me. She taught me to be courageous, to go forward and take action and be on good terms with everyone. This pushed me out of my comfort zone and made me take on tasks that went way beyond my normal job description and functional goals. Her motto was 'Make a good name for yourself and the family. Go forward in life and earn an honest income'.

These values imbued me with the ethics and integrity needed in any professional, and more so in a person in a high-level fiduciary position. These are essential qualities that no university teaches. Mother would encourage me to overcome fear and put myself out there. I thought of her when my CEO asked me to head the Safety, Health and Environment function, which I had no clue about. I thought of her at that point. My mother had left the comfort of her home in India and dared destiny by coming to this far away land of Malaya. How difficult could it be for me to take on a global director's position and lead the company in yield improvement and cost savings of millions of dollars?

While she never craved for fame or fortune, her encouragement to others to work for creating a good name for the family provided me with a seamless sense of self-esteem as I met top government officials and dignitaries. Her polite firmness in dealing with situations helped me when I was called upon to stand my ground during off-chance meetings with snarling creditors.

My achievements mean so much more to me because of the pride and joy they have brought to my mother who was always delighted to hear of an accomplishment by a member of the family.

When I had the distinct honour of meeting the Prime Minster of India over dinner, I thanked him for visiting our country and for doing all the great things that he was doing at home and abroad. His example, I have always felt, gives strength and determination to people across the world to strive and grow together. He replied in a very humble tone that it was his pleasure to meet and serve people. I was fascinated by the softness of his hands as I clasped them in mine. The very next thought I had was of my mother. How I wished she were present watching this special moment!

It pleased me to think what my mother would have felt, had she witnessed this exchange in person.

"Mom, this one is for you," I said.

Father and his gift of focus

I balanced my mother's teachings with my father's thoughts on the value of focus and discipline in carrying out one's duties, walking the narrow path, and staying out of trouble. His constant advice was to not to put my head where it was not needed. Having come from India, he had learnt the value of being street smart back home before he arrived in Malaya in the 1930s. He was a self-made man. He had come from very humble beginnings although he did say there was family land back in India, which was said to extend 'as far as the eyes could see'. He had come as a pioneer to make a new living in an unknown land and done very well for himself.

My father imparted many lessons on the right way of doing things. He taught me the value of balance in everything one did.

All the t's had to be crossed and all the i's had to be dotted. He had a keen head for numbers. I was just amazed by the way he would add up a set of thirty 8-digit numbers on a folio within a few seconds. He would not suffer fools and always expected common sense, honesty, timeliness, respect and results. My father's frugal ways have guided me in many ways. I feel that his professional rigor pervades my financial management techniques, cost reduction and cash flow planning.

I realized early on that we often take for granted the stability and nurturing we receive from our families. My father's disciplined way kept him very healthy. The way he controlled his food intake, his daily walks, his passion for sports and his enthusiasm for keeping abreast of the news taught me the value of living a balanced life. I understood that looking after myself was important if I wished to take care of others I cared about. This commitment to living a balanced life tells me how he lived such a rich life till the age of 97.

I envied his alert mind and the wisdom he had gathered.

It is almost magical that whenever I take a major action, choose or decide something, I always remember my father and his philosophy of action. His wisdom lives on in my heart and continues to direct my life.

I am fortunate to have been instructed by many gurus who have contributed to how I live my life, relate to people, work and pay back my dues to society. I am grateful that they have borne me on their shoulders and helped me become what I am today.

Brother Harold P. Reynolds

Brother Harold, the Australian principal of my secondary school, was one of the few people who took the trouble to pronounce my name correctly. More importantly, he remained youthful at heart all his life. His passion for the welfare of his students inspired The Class of '71 to meet and keep in touch with him on a regular basis for more than 50 years, wherever he was in any of the La Sallian Mission Schools worldwide. He used to say that life is sacred and that every life has meaning and purpose. He taught me the importance of reflection and the remarkable power of learning.

Sri Paramahamsa Yogananda

I was introduced to this Yogi in the early 1970's primarily through his book *The Autobiography Of A Yogi*. It had a profound impact for me. I understood the superiority of mind over body and of the soul over the mind. Those were my formative years. I merely took in the facts stated in the book back then. The real learning for me came when I entered early adulthood. I began to understand about overcoming evil by good. I also learned about sorrow, cruelty, kindness and ignorance. I still experience an awakening inside when I listen to this great Yogi speak on science, religion and realization over a century ago. I continue to read excerpts from his magical book to understand what it means to offer service to mankind or what is known in today's parlance as paying it forward.

Napoleon Hill

Napoleon Hill and his writings in general and *Think and Grow Rich* in particular are extraordinary revelations that brought to me many concepts beyond anything I had ever imagined. Reading the book over and over again brought me fresh insights and new perspectives that I could apply on an immediate basis. It is still amazing to know that the laws of success were researched in depth almost a hundred years ago and all of them are still relevant today despite our significantly changed times. This is a book I would recommend that people read at as early an age as possible.

It is a manuscript that many other success coaches have used as fodder to fuel their programs and careers.

Jack Canfield

One of the biggest projects in my life involved bringing my guru Jack Canfield to Malaysia for a two-day program in 2006. He had just published his book *The Success Principles*. He was excited to travel and talk about his 64 principles. He had agreed especially because I had earmarked one day for the youth. There is hardly a day when I do not apply any one of his precepts, be it visualization, E+R=O, taking 100% responsibility, or building one's success team. To talk about each of these principles and the impact they have had on my life would be one fat book in itself.

Robin Sharma

My brief meeting with Robin Sharma in Kuala Lumpur was charged with his overwhelming chemistry. He is such a fascinating personality. He speaks so simply and persuasively on how people should focus on all the good in their lives and think of ways to make things even better. I like how he expounds on the importance of eliminating the tyranny of impoverished thinking. I follow his guide to stand guard at the gate of my garden and only allow the very best information to enter. None of us can afford the luxury of a negative thought, not even one. A bit hard to do, but something we must!

I am done with my list for the purposes of this chapter but I am leaving out Sun Tzu, Mahatma Gandhi, Sadhguru Jaggi Vasudev, Daniel Goleman and Rumi for no reason other than the paucity of space. I find solace in the words of Paul Gardner as I leave this piece at a point where so many of my personal 'lighthouses' remain to be mentioned and so much I learned from them is being left unsaid:

A painting is never finished – it simply stops at interesting places.

Coming full circle, I conclude with the words of my mother, my first Guru: *"It is not how many years we live but what we do with them. It is not what we receive but what we give to others."*

Nara Subramaniam is a business and executive coach, financial consultant and trainer. With his wide-ranging experiences in the corporate world, he is now living his passion to build capacity and capability for entrepreneurs. He enjoys his mission to help people connect the dots while helping them transform to better manage the most misused resource, TIME. He is a proud member of MAPS which is affiliated with the GSF. He has now forayed into high impact virtual engagement and webinars.

www.resolveasia.com

resolveasia@gmail.com

All rights of this chapter held by Nara Subramaniam

7 MANTRAS OF ORGANIC SUCCESS

Living, working and changing radically in the digital age

BY VIJAYALAKSHMI RAMAN

Vijayalakshmi Raman is an original thinker, a creative writer, and a collaborative leader par excellence. I have personally learned so much from her. Her writings have a lot of practical insights and actionable takeaways. I find the simplicity in her writing very endearing. This piece is a must-read for anyone who aspires to lead a team.

Mahesh Narayan,
Senior Manager,
Accenture,
Bangalore

Chapter 5. Leading as if people matter

Collaborative Leadership (CL) is the way forward in a world that is being shaken and stirred by constant disruption caused by innovation as well as cataclysmic acts of God.

By Vijayalakshmi Raman

Collaborative leadership begins with the profound understanding that as humans we are interconnected beings with different strengths, capabilities, skills and temperaments. One can only do so much alone. He or she understands that our weaknesses can be compensated by the strengths of others and we on our part can help our colleagues, collaborators and co-workers achieve higher levels of productivity and success with the gifts we bring to the table.

In that sense collaborative leadership is like being the captain of a football team. The strengths of each member has to be recognized and each member has to be given charge of a particular area of the field with specific duties that helps them contribute optimally to the team success.

A collaborative leader will not just start a venture but also engage others in his vision and help others work together and be successful. He or she is the master of networking skills which is his greatest strength

He or she focuses more on the win–win mechanism. He builds a strong team that can face any situation. His colleagues never doubt themselves because they are guided by a strong collaborative leader. Closer home at a personal level, I used the principles of collaborative leadership instinctually when I was Senior Associate/Acting team lead at the Coimbatore Global Business Centre in the year 2014.

How of CL

Keep talking: One quality that a collaborative leader has to develop is the willingness to engage a wide variety of people in a conversation. I love talking to people hailing from different places and backgrounds. In my own practice of collaborative leadership, I try to understand the culture of my team even when it is spread across geographical locations. I make efforts to understand the geography of the area, the climate, special cuisines and things well-known about that place. Such conversations engage them. It helps me build much-needed rapport. This made my onshore counterparts very comfortable with me right from the principal stakeholder to the junior most associate

Motivating skills: Collaborative leaders motivate teams to create more value for themselves as well as their stakeholders. They utilise transferable skills like stakeholder management, strategic planning, and quantitive analysis in their leadership style

Horizontal leadership: They make a clean break from the hierarchical mindset and inculcated an open culture instead, where colleagues help each other and make cross-functional relationships possible. Such leaders encourage constructive conflicts that bring out the best out of people by kindling the spirit of competition and encourage the sharing of information openly. Both traits power the growth of the organisations they lead.

Contextual Intelligence: Contextual intelligence is practical-know-how acquired indirectly. It is not possible to know and understand everything about every process in one's company but one does have a grasp of the value of a particular department or person in the company at large. A collaborative leader not only possesses high contextual intelligence he is respectful of the contributions of each participant in the overall processes in the organsation.

Attitude to risk: They are risk-takers, innovators, creators and all these behaviors result in growth for themselves as well as their company and other stakeholders. We live in an age of contant disruption cause by innovaton as well as 'acts of God'. Collaborative leadership is the key to handling this turbulance. Every individual's skill has to be taken into account when one responds to the latest disruption.

High emotional, social and crisis quotient: One needs resilience for handling a new initiative. In a time of great storms, flexibility has become mandatory. A leader heading an organisation or team has to undertake collaborative initiatives among   employees and listen actively during meetings.

Non-charismatic style: This is not a necessary condition for being a collaborative leader but calm, collected and understated people make for very good collaborative leaders. In a world that looks up to charismatic leaders, such a leader could even be boring while being very strong within their knowledge area. He or she creates a collaborative environment where people with purpose, clear vision, and set of values unite.

Coming back to my adventure of wearing the hat of a collaborative leader, I chose to steer newly joined team members as they faced initial challenges in our company, where our workday rarely ended with eight hours of work. My stakeholder management skills helped me become the acting supervisor here to communicate, coordinate and deliver what was expected out of our team in a much more effective and efficient way.

I was a strong believer of informal meetings. Hence, I organised them as and when required, so that the team was well-informed with the latest updates and upgradations. 'Doing more with less' was the principle used with this team.

The tools we used to keep this collaborative process were as follows:

1) A centralized storing of documents which were accessible to both our GBC team as well as the stakeholder.
2) Whenever, there was a major noticeable process change, virtual meetings were setup and we discussed the possible outcomes, hits and misses.

To summarize, here are the areas one must work on constantly to be a good collaborative leader:

1) Networking Skills
2) Influencing Skills
3) Balanced Motivating skills
4) Strategic planning
5) Stakeholder management
6) Quantitative Analysis

All said, collaborative leadership is the way forward to achieve organic success in this world driven by competition. So let us start collaborating and supporting each other's and grow together to new heights every day.

Vijayalakshmi Raman is a Master Black Belt Trained Operations Specialist, Data Science enthusiast, an aspiring Author, and a coach. She is a proud protégé of JJ School of Employability. She has a mission to help Working women manage their Work Life Balance and to find that extra time for their personal growth.

vijayalakshmi.raman45@gmail.com

All rights of this chapter held by Vijayalakshmi Raman

7 MANTRAS OF ORGANIC SUCCESS

*Living, working and changing radically
in the digital age*

BY JITENDRA NATH MAHATO

I know **Jitendra Nath Mahato** since when he was a high school student. Even as an adolescent, he was different from his friends. His thoughts were mature, he was full of ideas and had a fixed goal. He had great ambitions.

He has marched forward in life but has not forgotten his high school teachers. This tells us what a remarkable person he is.

I congratulate him on the publication of his first book 7 *Mantras of Organic Success*. He has my blessings!

Atashi Ghosh
PGT (English)
Senior teacher, CBSE School
Jamshedpur.

Chapter 6. Beyond schools for clerks and servants

India has been a free nation for over 70 years but our education system is yet to break free from the chains in which it was bound by the British East India Company in the 1750s

By Jitendra Nath Mahato

We Indians are proud of our ancient educational heritage. The Gurukulas were famous at one point of time and students from all corners of the country and even abroad came to study in these Gurukulas and Mahavidyalayas. Traditionally, a man's life was divided into four stages – Brahmacharya, Grihastha, Vanaprastha and Sanyasa. Each stage was generally of 25 years. The first stage of Bhramacharya was generally spent in the Gurukulas where students would stay with their Gurus or Acharyas far away from the hustle and bustle of the populated areas separated from their parents. The wife of Guru was accorded the status of a mother by the students who lived with the Guru and his family. Kings and parents of students would provide funds required for the operation of the Gurukulas or Ashramas. The four Vedas, Upanishads, Itihasas and works of literature, grammar, poetics and performing arts were authored by ancient Indians who were taught in this system. In exchange for their learning, students gave Gurudakshina as a token of their gratitude at the end of their education in various forms of services or in kind.

But with the Islamic invasion of India, the Gurukula system of education declined. It is telling that in 1193 the invader, Bakhtiyar Khilji disturbed by the fact that an Indian scholar and teacher knew more than his own men, decided to destroy the roots of secular knowledge, Buddhism and Ayurveda. He set fire to the great library of Nalanda and burned down nearly nine million manuscripts.

Twelve hundred years after the invasions that marked the establishment of Islamic power in India, the era of European colonisation began. During the colonial period, even the remnants of the Gurukula system that had survived in some parts of India witnessed a complete rout as patronage declined with farmers and artisans got impoverished due to high taxation and import of cheap British products into the Indian market. It suited the East India Company rulers to enforce a new system of education in India that would provide them with the Indian clerks and sepoys needed to administrate the country on behalf of the Europeans. This killed whatever remained of the Indian system of education and values.

The East India Company brought English Education into the country. Till India's freedom in 1947, these institutions were completely managed by the European Missionaries. After Independence the management was handed over to the care of the Anglo-Indian community. By then, the complete ancient history of the Indians was obliterated from the consciousness of Indians and they were taught the history of the Europeans and the Americans. Social reformers like Dayananda Saraswati, the founder of Arya Samaj and Swami Shraddhanand, were the pioneers of the modern Gurukula system, who in 1886 founded now-widespread Dayanand Anglo-Vedic Public Schools and Universities. Sri Sri Ravi Shankar also maintains a Gurukula at the Art of Living centre in Bangalore. Sri Aurobindo started the Aurobindo Ashram in Puducherry post his retirement from active politics to revive the study of the Vedas, which the ancient Indians help in great reverence.

More than seven decades post our Independence have passed. Unfortunately, we continue to follow the same old colonial education system left behind by the British East India Company. The different states run their own state board education syllabus, while there are two central boards – Central Board of Secondary Education and an Anglo-Indian run board Council for the Indian School Certificate Examinations.

Importantly, all existing boards continue to follow the pattern of education outlined by the East India Company. The current Education system is producing students with more theoretical concepts than those with practical and professional skills. Even if a student has a masters or PhD degree, they do not possess any life skills to earn their livelihood. When these 'graduates' are taken into a company or a government sector, they have to be fully trained in order to perform any work. Most students lack interest in the subjects in which they hold degrees. Because of the lack of useful skills, such highly qualified Indian youths find themselves jobless in an economy where there are a lot of jobs. Students forced into engineering and medical schools by their parents do not make enthusiastic employees. Boys are mainly asked to pursue engineering. Girls are herded into the medical profession. This gives birth to a lot of frustrations and unrest in the people. Even if the youth somehow manage to bag jobs due to their high scores and glittering degrees, they are not able to fulfil their responsibilities or execute tasks entrusted to them. Also, since the supply of educated youth is rising and demand is low, remuneration has not increased much if one factors in the rate of inflation. This is raising the frustration levels of the youth who are pushed towards suicide and mental health conditions. Athletically inclined youth who can excel at sports are being forced into academics. Those who are keen on pursuing medicine are being pushed into engineering.

We need reform in our education system before it's too late. There are seven main areas where educational reforms are required in India. They are as follows:

i. Rote learning
ii. Evaluation system
iii. Equal respect to all the subjects
iv. Better training of educators
v. Introduction of technology
vi. Personalization of education

vii.   Purpose of education

The new education system should be more practical. It should be oriented towards teaching life skills, technical skills, soft skills, behavioural skills, management skills and financial skills. There should be a scientific evaluation of students, which reveals the passions and interest areas of students from the elementary stage of education onward. These evaluations may include psychometric analysis, NLP based counselling, and questionnaires based counselling. Only after such an evaluation has been undertaken should the student be trained in areas he or she reveals inclination for. This should be an additional area of education beyond general scholastics. Parents need to be counselled on the importance of these areas so they support the campaign to create such a new educational system for the betterment of their children. There should be regular counselling starting from the students of standard one till they matriculate. Some students could be good at sports, some others in engineering, and yet others in the field of medicine, music, arts, and crafts.

These steps need to be urgently taken if we are to raise good citizens in this country of ours. Countries like Japan and South Korea are handling these challenges much better. The Indian government should analyse the reasons for the dismal state of our youth and consider educational reforms. In 1993 and 2009, the Yashpal Committee under Prof Yashpal offered some recommendations to the Indian government. Only some of the recommendations have been implemented so far. Major reforms are yet to BE taken.

We need to revive a school system that is based on our ancient Gurukulas system. Students would be trained within its four walls in areas aligned with their passion, interests, and skill. The teachers themselves should be trained sufficiently to train students in their respective skill areas. We should revisit the value based education that we had earlier.

Work has already started in this direction with the help of principals of different schools, professors of colleges and the educationists working on various new paradigms.

I hope we receive the support of the Indian Government for the necessary approvals and the implementation as well. The politicisation of this alarming issue should be avoided. I need the support of parents' as well as students' associations across the nation. Let us pledge that the tomorrow will bring in an education system that is better aligned to our culture, heritage and aspiration to make India an economic superpower.

Jitendra Nath Mahato is an IT Professional with around one-and-a-half decade of Industry exposure in IT, Manufacturing and Embedded Systems. He is a Speaker and Coach and currently started working in the educational reforms in the nation. He is the Past President of Rotaract Club of Bangalore – 2010-11. Rotaract is the youth wing of Rotary International. His major project was AARAMBH- State Level Sports meet for the especially abled children of Karnataka at Sree Kanteerava Stadium on 19th Feb 2011 during his tenure.

jitendra.jitu16@gmail.com

7 MANTRAS OF ORGANIC SUCCESS

*Living, working and changing radically
in the digital age*

BY J LAKSHMINARAYANAN

I have been associated **with J Lakshminarayanan** for more than 11 years. He is an astute finance leader who is result oriented and one with excellent interpersonal skills. I am happy to see him pen down his vast experience and share insights on career. Wish him the best to write on more topics in the future

M Subash,
Dell India.

Chapter 7. From Appa with love

My 10 principles of succeeding in the workplace for the strong, confident, kind, and happy young women I know my two princesses will grow up to become

By J Lakshminarayanan

Dear Daughters,

You are just 11 and 7 in the year I type these words. Much of what I am sharing is beyond your playful minds. It is an important role of parents to be life coaches because most of us go through life without knowing or realising the importance of mentors or coaches in our careers. My purpose of writing this article is to share my experience, which I hope will act as a guide when you step into your own chosen careers a few years from now!

I was born in a conservative middle-class family, and grew up in Vellore, a town 140 kilometres from Chennai. I subsequently moved to Chennai to complete my education following which I began my career. An introvert by nature, I used to hesitate to express myself unless I felt certain that I belonged among the people around me. I had developed an inferiority complex inside because I was a boy from a small town who had moved to huge city like Chennai. There was much here that had to be handled differently from the town I had left behind. Despite such a complexity, I did excel at academics and studied hard to become a chartered accountant. I began my career as an officer in a non-banking financial company and worked my way up to become a senior manager of a large fortune 100 company with several of my colleagues reporting me. This journey was not smooth. It was filled with highs and lows. I had rough patches and smooth sailings. I have often, hesitated, faltered, and failed. However, in the end, after every fall, I just raised myself up, dusted my clothes and walked on.

My purpose of writing this piece is to share the lessons I have learned along the way, sometimes at great cost. That is not to say that you two do not have the right to your own mistakes.

You do.

This is just an attempt to have a conversation with the beautiful young women you will become, and I hope that at least some part of the conversation will prove to be of value to you. These are insights gathered from 18+ years of my professional adventure is a gift of love from your Appa:

1.   Expect a clash of personalities

A conflicting situation may arise between the nature of an individual and what behavioural pattern is expected at workplace. You are not alone in this as many individuals face this challenge. I was not as communicative or organized a person in the initial part of my career. This is something that changed over the years. My ability to lead and influence people was gained over a period. People do shape themselves by sharpening their strengths and addressing their weak links in their career journeys. It is important to work on these on a consistent basis.

2.   Build your credibility. Build your brand

Employees are hired based on the idea they manage to convey of skillsets during the job interview. Those who show the *promise* of delivering are hired. The real test happens *when the rubber hits the road*. It is incredibly important to be a consistent performer in the initial years to establish your credibility and establish your brand. It is important to keep adding value to the organization while keeping the career objective clear and concise. Remember that the credibility and brand building are ongoing exercises and one does not stop because one has reached a level.

3. Competition

I have experienced peer pressure in situations where colleagues have outperformed me and when I have outperformed others. I realized over the years that the competition is not there outside but within. I needed to compete with myself. This ensures that I become better than I am today. Healthy competition is to be considered an opportunity to enhance oneself. Active cultivation of this approach has helped me progress in my career!

4. Art of saying 'no'

I was given some tasks at the initial part of my career that were way more complex than I anticipated when I accepted them. I lacked experience. Saying "yes" comes easily to me because that is a personality trait. Later, I realized that I could have asked questions to gather data points and be well informed before either saying 'yes' or 'no". Such a situation is likely to arise in your career as well. Ensure that you carefully evaluate all the relevant factors before you utter that 'yes'. Do not be pressured into taking a hasty decision. Make informed choices.

*In the famous words of Tony Blair, "The **art** of leadership is **saying no**, not **saying yes**. It is very easy to **say yes**". The skill of **saying no** develops over the course of time.*

5. Leadership

Leadership may or may not be associated with job title or position. There may be situations where you are required to take charge of a situation. If you can inspire or influence people by executing things, there is a leader in you. It took me several years to realize this. If you realize that you can make a difference to a person or process, nurture that. It eventually grows to make you an inspiring and influential leader over time. It is also important to lead a task (not related to work like CSR, Team building, etc), which is of interest to the larger team or organization. Consider it your professional gym for developing leadership muscle.

6.   Leading without authority

Over years, I have been tasked with handling a few projects that were significant for the organization. These tasks were of the nature that I had to get things done from others who were not in reporting relationships with me. More so, they were not in the department that I was part of. Apart from the personality challenges that I had issues dealing with, I also realized that there were some special skills required to handle the projects. This called for leading without authority. A Forbes article published in May 2017 titled *3 Crucial Skills for Leading without Authority*' is worth referring. I expect it to be relevant for all time. Here are the skills they said must be employed to lead the project without authority:

> i.   **Empathetic listening**
> ii.   **Warm body language**
> iii.   **Positive emotions**

7.   Relationships

As in every walk of life, building strong relationship is important in the corporate world too. It is also referred to as networking. Stronger the network, better your net worth. As an introvert, I developed aversion in the initial few year of career to networking because it does not come naturally to me. However, I started to note that my interpersonal skills were so strong within my circle. It made me to realize that if I expanded my circle through networking, I could influence more people with my interpersonal skills. The limitation of being an introvert was no longer relevant when I gradually started to expand my network. Taking constant action to talk to people without feeling the pressure of being pushed is the best way to expand the network and create relationships.

8. Job rotation

Most organizations invest time and effort in employee development through trainings and job rotations within. It is equally important for individuals to have a development plan with specific focus on the following areas:

    i.   **Education and experience**
    ii.   **Existing skills and strengths (technical and soft)**
    iii.   **New skills and opportunities (technical and soft)**
    iv.   **Next possible role for rotation**

This plan provides clarity on the direction that an individual wishes to take. Rotating an employee to different roles is a lot easier early in the career. As one rises, the number of roles are reduced. It is lonelier at the top, making job rotation challenging (due to stiff competition and skill gaps). I realized with experience that job rotation is difficult in vertical organization that are the norm in large corporations. Moving from one role to another can only happen for a seasoned individual with a lot of planning and meticulous execution.

9. Asking for help

Asking for help is another art that you must learn. How to ask for help without feeling weird? One learns with experience when to ask for help, how to ask and whom to ask. I am still trying to master this even after 18+ years of work life. I am not talking about minor assistance in performing tasks that are easier to handle. The focus here is on mentorship needed to steer the career, strengthen existing skills, adding new skills, and working on behavioural aspects. Many organizations come up with mentorship programmes that benefit both parties – mentors and mentees. This is a great platform to develop the muscle for seeking help. Remember that even world champions need coaches!

10. Technological advancement

I recall that I used work in a custom-made local accounting system at the beginning of my career. With the advent of technology, I started to work on ERP systems after going through the necessary trainings. We are in the middle of Industrial Revolution 4.0 with technological changes happening at break-neck speed. It is essential to keep pace with mastering digital platforms / technologies. A recent study says that today's students may be working in jobs that have not yet been created. It is difficult to predict the nature of the workplaces of the future, but a few things are clear. Be adaptable. Master new technologies and change course if the situation demands it. Be open to creating alternate careers if your old career is not a place of abundance anymore.

I would like to leave you with the following concepts that I got introduced to recently. Both are profound and would guide you on career choices (Employment or Entrepreneurship) as you go along:

A. The Japanese IKIGAI concept explores the following areas:

    i. What do you LOVE?
    ii. What are you GOOD AT?
    iii. What the world NEEDS?
    iv. What can you be PAID FOR?

B. Simon Sinek's 'Golden Circle'

The **Golden Circle** is a **concept** developed by Simon Sinek who says, 'People don't buy what you do, they buy why you do it.' According to Sinek, most people communicate by starting with the "what" they do aspect and eventually work their way back to talk about "how" and "why" they do what they do.

So, that will be all for now. I know it ends suddenly. I am aware that it is an unfinished conversation but then when is a father done talking to his daughters?

Never.

Stay strong, girls!

Love,

Appa.

J Lakshminarayanan is a Chartered Accountant who has had a flourishing career with a couple of Fortune 100 companies for about 18 years. He is an inspirational leader known for his sound accounting and internal controls expertise. His leadership style involves a people-oriented approach, hands-on stakeholder management, humility and a positive mind set.

All rights of this chapter held by J Lakshminarayanan

7 MANTRAS OF ORGANIC SUCCESS

*Living, working and changing radically
in the digital age*

BY JOGESH JAIN

End note: My 'why?'

You have to discover why you were born and dedicate yourself to it if you wish to achieve greatness

By Jogesh Jain

I still remember 2010, when one of my friends came to me and suggested that we should be doing something beyond earning a salary in a 9-5 job.

After researching different options, we decided to start a coaching centre for commerce students. It all started with a thought and in the first year we managed to attract seven students.

All our students passed with good grades. In three years, we grew to a point where we were raking in a monthly revenue of Rs. 1.5 lakh.

Everything was going well, but my commitments in my day job kept growing with time, and I had to exit my business.

This was not an easy decision.

Not to be defeated, I then started an accounting and income tax business. This enterprise picked up well. I built a client base of 80 in a short time.

I did not continue with this business for too long. Somewhere, there was a disconnect. My next venture was selling fruit juice. I also began teaching at a coaching academy.

As the months rolled by, I felt a monotony setting in. I wasn't feeling enthusiastic about what I was doing. I realised that I had only been starting new businesses for the sake of making more money. This one-track focus on cash was not enough. No wonder, I was losing interest in it so fast.

I was just not passionate about my businesses. I was merely conforming to the culture around me. Instead of questioning the way things were being done, I was becoming one with them. And by doing so, I was relegating myself to mediocrity, to scarcity, to a limited life experience.

Around this time, I began noticing how newcomers in my multinational company were finding it difficult to adjust to the demanding work culture. I knew what was required to help them make the transition but this was not a part of my mandate. Moreover, my own responsibilities were substantial. I had little room to add to my work. I remained stuck in this uncomfortable position for six years. I knew I could help but found myself unable to. A day came when I decided to break free.

It dawned upon me that my passion was helping employees become employable.

If you see yourself in such a depressing situation and feel that the people who surround you are not working to help you move forward toward your passion, try disconnecting with them for 10 days to arrive at the clarity of thoughts, clarity of goals, and clarity of action to help you move in the desired direction.

I realised for myself that teaching people, and coaching them, gave me a feeling that I was paying it forward. I have always found joy in helping others. Whenever I would share my new ideas with my wife, she would say "You are so energetic and enthusiastic and never sit silently at one place." Her encouragement gave me the boost and the push to experiment some more.

Questioning the status quo

When I started coaching, we were living in Dombivli, which was a 90-minute commute to work. It amazed me to see people traveling daily in the same train with same set of people and at the same time for their entire lives.

It made me wonder.

"Don't they get bored?"

"How do they manage to stay so happy despite everything?"

I was finding it extremely tough to convince myself to catch the same train at the same place and with the same people. I just could not come to terms with being so 'motor minded'.

I started asking a lot of question about life and life purpose to myself. I became a rebel. I questioned everything I saw. Right from doing my job to paying my bills to subjects like happiness and fulfilment.

Have you pondered over these questions yourself?

I have observed people with 10+ years of work experience who more often than not find themselves facing a mid-career crisis.

Almost every third individual entering the bracket of senior management toys with the idea of starting a business of his or her own. However, due to one challenge or the other, the decision is shelved and the desired shift just does not happen.

After every session of my free career guidance sessions, my students would come to me and say, "Sir, I relate so much to what you just said. I could connect with you. Thank you for sharing this. It has helped me to understand things better."

Such feedback has encouraged me to research the subject further, and develop my muscles in the field of career guidance. It helped me keep abreast of the latest happenings in the market.

My search for an answer

They say there are two dates which are important in your life. One is the day you are born. The other day is when you know 'why' you were born.

I wanted to know my 'why?'.

It is not common for most people to seek an answer to this question. Most die without even knowing that they might have an all-powerful but undiscovered 'why'!

This was when I stopped living my 'motor-mind lifestyle', which included working in the same company, with the same boss, boarding the same train to work, and sitting at the same place while travelling.

A close friend called me around this time.

"I quit my job," he said.

This got me thinking.

Could I quit my job too?

I took me almost two years to take the plunge. I had been teaching students and had been helping them design their resumes, create effective LinkedIn profiles, and coaching them to negotiate their salaries. After some thinking, I decided that this is what I would do henceforth. I quit my job and began my entrepreneurship journey in the career guidance industry.

If you have been contemplating moving from being an employee to an entrepreneur like me, here is my message:

Dream big. Be an action taker. Become an entrepreneur.